IMAGES
of England

RADFORD

Wollaton Road School, 1938. This school was certainly here in 1893 when Miss M. Palfree was the headmistress. Additional outbuildings were added in 1894. The school was built next to the old road to Wollaton and Trowell. In the 1930s, this building was adjacent to the Nottingham Car Dismantling Depot. Some names which have been supplied with this picture include: Alan Sisson, Abi Smith, Peter Bywater, Ken Smith, Roy Davis, Jim Beasley, Alice Savage, Alan Dean, Doug Gregory, Peter Davis, Ken Morris, Jack Morris.

Compiled by
Chris Richards

First published 2001

Tempus Publishing Limited
The Mill, Brimscombe Port,
Stroud, Gloucestershire, GL5 2QG

ISBN 0 7524 2174 3

Typesetting and origination by
Tempus Publishing Limited
Printed in Great Britain by
Midway Clark Printing, Wiltshire

This book is dedicated to my late parents, Lisa and Harry Richards.

A class at Forster Street School, *c*. 1957. This photograph would have been taken in the yard behind the wall seen on p. 25. The master on the right is Mr Woods.

Contents

Acknowledgements

I would like to thank everyone who has encouraged me during my research and supplied stories and photographs: Paul Fillingham, Keith and the Dudley family, Alan Marshall, John Robey, Evelyn Broughton, Ernie and Lil Boseley, Joyce Mollart, Valerie A. Stanley and the Radford Local History Society, Jim Diack, Brian Sillitoe, Florence and Bert Newton, Valerie Fearn, Michael Clarke, Ron Thorne, Ray and Kath Brookes, Robert Thorne, Paul Saxton, George Colley, Peter Koschmann, Joyce Swinscoe, Peter Walker and Dennis and Anne Hall. I wish to express my gratitude to all the staff of the Nottingham Local Studies Library, the Robert Shaw Primary School, Raleigh Industries, Imperial Tobacco and John Player & Sons. Also, thanks to Paul Molde and the Riley studio for their support and advice.

My thanks also to my wife Debbie for being patient during the long lonely hours of research and to my father-in-law John Neagle for being both chauffeur and historian during this project.

The frontage of Raleigh Industries, Triumph Road, 1992. When this factory was built in 1952, it joined the premises of Conflow Ltd, valve manufacturers, the Woolpack Hosiery Works and the Ceylon Tea Growers' Association, who all had businesses on this road.

Introduction

The District of Radford is located to the west of the City of Nottingham, and was almost certainly named after the abundance of sandstone rock where the Alfreton Road crossed the River Leen by a ford, giving rise to the name 'red-ford'. There is mention of a place in the Nottingham area called Redeford in the 1100s, the original village being based around the St Peter's Street area, where a church was established.

It is said that the White Horse Inn on Ilkeston Road existed in the 1660s. By the eighteenth century, the Ilkeston, Derby and Alfreton Roads had been established, and in the late 1790s Benjamin Darker had begun building houses on Burke Street. Radford's population in 1801 was 2,269 and in 1831 had quadrupled to 9,806. By 1871 the figure had risen to 15,127, larger even than the town of Newark. This was mainly due to the rapid growth of the lace industry in the early nineteenth century. By 1901, Radford's population had increased further to 35,500.

At the beginning of the twentieth century the two main Radford industries began to take a hold. The Raleigh Cycle Company and John Player & Sons' tobacco factories dominated the skyline, and along with lace and hosiery manufacture, coal and ironworks, were the main employers of local people. In 1900, the two main Radford landowners were Lord Middleton and William Wilson.

A glance at a map of Radford from 1908 shows the Radford Colliery up towards Bobber's Mill, and Radford railway station just off Canterbury Road. Some colourful Radford street names could also be found around this time – Nut Yard, Pleasant Place, Victory Yard, Chew's Yard, Cherry Square, Sunburn Terrace, Pelican Place and Stilton Terrace. Many varied businesses existed side by side in Radford. A brief look at Denman Street in 1902 shows cabinet makers, milk dealers, tea merchants, fish friers, music teachers, painters, cow keepers and pie makers, all within a few hundred yards of each other.

By 1957, a new extension to the Raleigh cycle factory had been built on Wollaton Road, coinciding with the clearance of some of the houses in the St Peter's Street area. The early 1960s saw the Mitchell Street/Edinburgh Street area redeveloped, with modern high-rise flats built to replace the maze of terraced streets that had grown too old for any sort of habitation. New flats, such as Connaught and Denman Gardens, were named after the streets they replaced.

I have lived in the area since I was born in 1962, the son of a Raleigh Cycle factory worker. For the first three years of my life we lived at 20 Pine Street, Radford. The area was condemned in 1965 and we were re-located to a council house less than half a mile away. My father was always telling stories, not only of the back-to-back housing and community spirit, but the grinding poverty and struggle that was 1930s Radford. My father Harry Richards had been, like his father and grandfather, a manual labourer.

Upon starting a three-year design and photography degree course in 1980 at Liverpool Polytechnic, I acquired my first SLR camera, a Pentax K1000, and returned home at weekends to record the area and its changing landscape. By summer 1980, demolition work had already begun in the Denman Street area, taking out the central section of what, in the 1950s, had been a lavish parade of shops. These stretched all the way from St Peter's Street to Canning Circus, catering to every need of the shopper.

I knew that I had to capture it all on film before it was too late. My parents always encouraged me to record as much as I could. I would often get up at 3 a.m. to catch the summer morning light on the ancient brickwork, and sometimes walk the streets all day long, turning corner after corner, picking out whatever images appealed to my teenage sensibility.

In particular, the area bounded by Hartley Road, Radford Boulevard, Denman Street and Norton Street was savagely attacked by the bulldozers, acquiring a Somme-like desolation before it was redeveloped in the mid 1980s. Whole rows of streets were removed systematically, the pale yellow lights of shops and public houses cutting through the twilight, the only buildings left untouched in a sea of bricks and timber. Most of the photographs depicting snow and fog were taken in sub-zero temperatures. Walking on sheets of ice, my fingers almost froze to the camera body, and cobbled streets coated with black ice were especially treacherous!

In the 1980s, almost all Radford public houses displayed a 'Shipstones' or 'Home Ales' sign, the two local breweries that are now sadly no more. The local pubs did a brisk trade with the twin industries of Raleigh and Player's, and Friday and Saturday nights were always guaranteed to be lively ones.

It was rumoured that the Raleigh factory on Faraday Road was to be demolished at the end of 1989. This building, with its famous 'Raleigh Cycle Company' lettering, had always been visible from the train when I returned home to photograph my home town. By 1991 the demolition crews had flattened the entire factory, from Salisbury Street to Cycle Road, and work had started on the foundations of a new housing estate.

Many local landmarks have now gone forever – the giant Raleigh factory clock on the Faraday Road bridge, the beautifully ornate John Player tobacco factory entrance on Beckenham Road, the Barnetts Sweet Factory on Hartley Road, and the Grundy Athletic Club next to the Boulevard Hotel. Radford taverns like the Balaclava Hero, Denman Inn, Phoenix, Polish Lancer, Three Tuns, Cherry Tree Inn, Bugle Horn, Pelican and White Swan have all long since vanished.

However, new buildings have emerged to replace the old, and the area is now being extensively improved. The old buildings are now being carefully refurbished, a far cry from the ruthless demolition programme of the 1960s. At the time of writing, more construction work is now in progress on Alfreton Road and on new college buildings to join the new multi-million pound Jubilee Campus on Wollaton Road. This work continues, with several substantial regeneration programmes now under way, to take Radford into the twenty-first century.

One
Early Days

Eretta Shaw outside 20 Pine Street, 1914. Born in 1862, she celebrated her hundredth birthday at Rothesay Avenue, Lenton. Eretta was a Pine Street resident well into her nineties. In the 1940s, her granddaughter Evelyn Broughton was one of the famous 'Player's Angels', who made the Player's cigarettes by hand.

Madge, Harry and Albert Richards, 36 Schooner Street, 1930s. Schooner Street consisted mainly of simple dwellings, with one downstairs room, one bedroom and an attic room, with cold water taps plumbed into an open courtyard. No. 48 housed the tiny Bugle Horn alehouse, known locally as 'The Nick'. Its last licensee, in 1966, was J.H. Hopkins.

Drinking at the Midland Hotel, 1950s. Annie Pearson is seen on the far right, the wife of local window cleaner Frank Pearson, who lived at 56 Kennington Road. This public house, on Wollaton Road, lives on today as the renamed Handle Bar.

Chris Richards with rhubarb, 20 Pine Street, 1964. The typical terraced house yard at this time contained an outside lavatory, tin bath and lots of concrete. However, the more resourceful tenants would dig out a section and plant vegetables, rhubarb being one of them.

Below: Two views of Maurice Kirby's coal and wood yard, 322 Denman Street, 1930s. This business faced Cheetham's Stores on Dulwich Road, and existed right up until the property was knocked down in 1980. The ancient sign on the brickwork is advertising Zebo Liquid Black Grate Polish. The couple in the pictures are Mr and Mrs Kirby. On the left is a stray dog that was a regular visitor to shops in the area.

Cheetham's Stores, 320 Denman Street, 1950s. Alan Marshall is proudly displaying a friend's greyhound on Dulwich Road. Cheetham's was listed in the early 1880s as being a grocer's shop, but by 1950 had been taken over by Jack Barlow. Another grocer's in the area, Cowpertwait's, boasted stuffed Pekinese dogs inside the shop. Cheetham's Stores was demolished in 1980.

Girls on Kennington Road in 1951. From left to right, they are: Shirley Pearson, Jean Rimes (nicknamed Babs) and Maureen Pearson. The Pearson sisters lived at No. 56. In the 1950s this road had three grocer's shops, belonging to Gordon Harris, Olive Smith and John Wright. No. 95 Kennington Road was home to Bannister's barbers.

Man on a moped, Dulwich Road, 1963. This view is looking down towards Norwood Road. In the 1960s, Raleigh Industries produced the popular Supermatic, Mark Two and Roma mopeds. The rider is Maurice Kirby, owner of the nearby coal yard. Toone's card and paper merchants is the large building on the left.

VE Day celebrations, Wollaton Road, 1945. The giant Player's Bonded Warehouses, painted in camouflage colours during the war, are on the left. The original gaslights are still in existence, as are the electric lines for the trams. Wollaton Road Mixed Board School is the building on the right.

Radford YMCA and Boys' Brigade football teams, 1949. Back row: the YMCA football team in the NABC League. Middle row: the Boys' Brigade football team. Front row: the Boys' Brigade PE team. The teams are posing in front of the YMCA building on Grant Street. Etched in chalk on the gate behind the teams is 'key at 27 Denton Street', the home of Donald Hewitt. Another popular local football team was the Radford East End Colts.

Brian Dudley, Denman Street, 1950s. Brian was the son of Denman Street chip shop owner Tommy Dudley, who kept a shop at No. 95. In 1956 this street had over seven fried fish establishments including Seston's, Skill's, Cockayne's and Fiori Fiore's. Tommy's shop was pulled down as part of the slum clearance programme of 1966.

Harry Richards at a snooker match in the Boulevard Hotel, Radford Boulevard, 1956. A full-size snooker table was, along with a dartboard, an essential item in some pubs in this area. Radford, Gregory and Lenton Boulevards were constructed in the 1880s. This pub dates from 1883.

Lisa Richards, Pine Street, 1957. Numbers 1, 3 and 5 Pine Street can be seen in the distance. At the end of the road, at 247-251 Ilkeston Road, was Smith's Bakery, which sold 'Nelson Squares', pastries with a tasty filling of bread and fruit. In 1894, 17 and 19 Pine Street and 10 and 11 Holland Place were sold for a total of £179.

Soldier's release book from 1946, issued to demobilized soldiers following the end of the Second World War. The official stamp from the post office at 310 Ilkeston Road can be seen on the cover. The post office was also a chemist's shop and was next to Ilkeston Road Picture House, which opened in 1914 and became the Goldmine Bingo Hall in 1960.

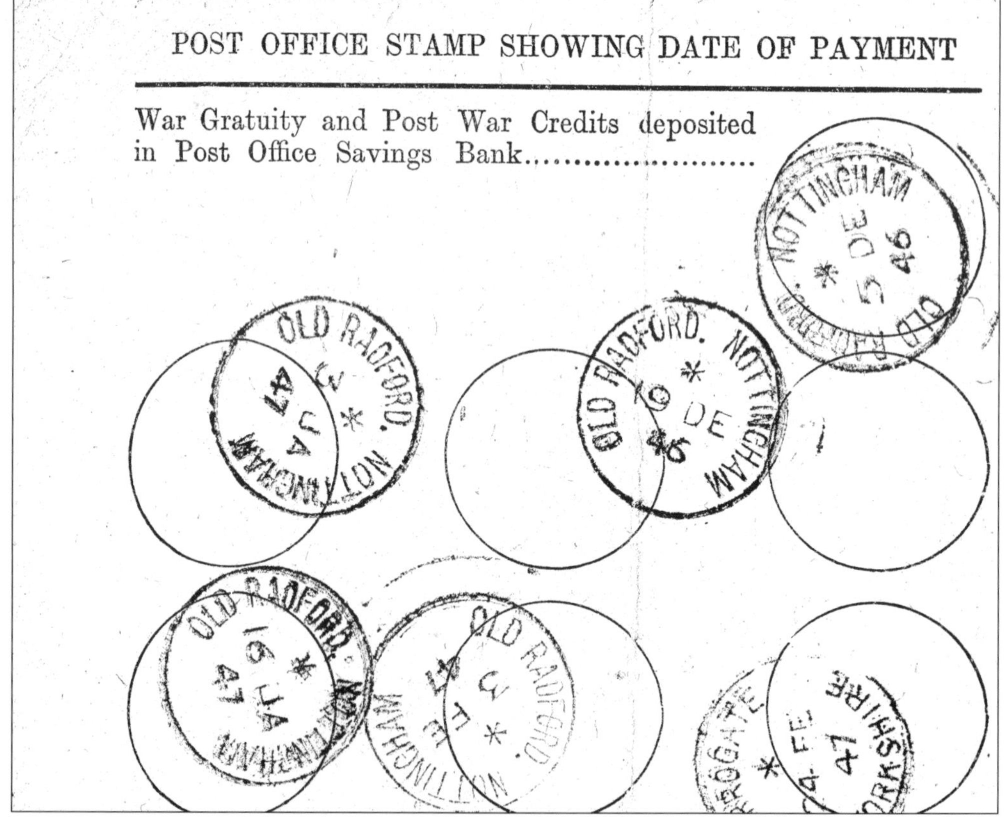

POST OFFICE STAMP SHOWING DATE OF PAYMENT

War Gratuity and Post War Credits deposited in Post Office Savings Bank.......................

The back yard of 267 Denman Street, 1960. This property was next to the Forster Street School, facing Kirby's coal yard and Cheetham's Stores. The house was previously occupied by J. Drayton, watchmaker, but around 1900 had been Beeton's men's hairdresser and tobacconists. The Radford back yards became storage areas for all manner of items, including mangles, tools, pigeons, canaries and bicycles. From left to right: Barry Brown, David Roberts and Alan Marshall, whose father Samuel was the tenant.

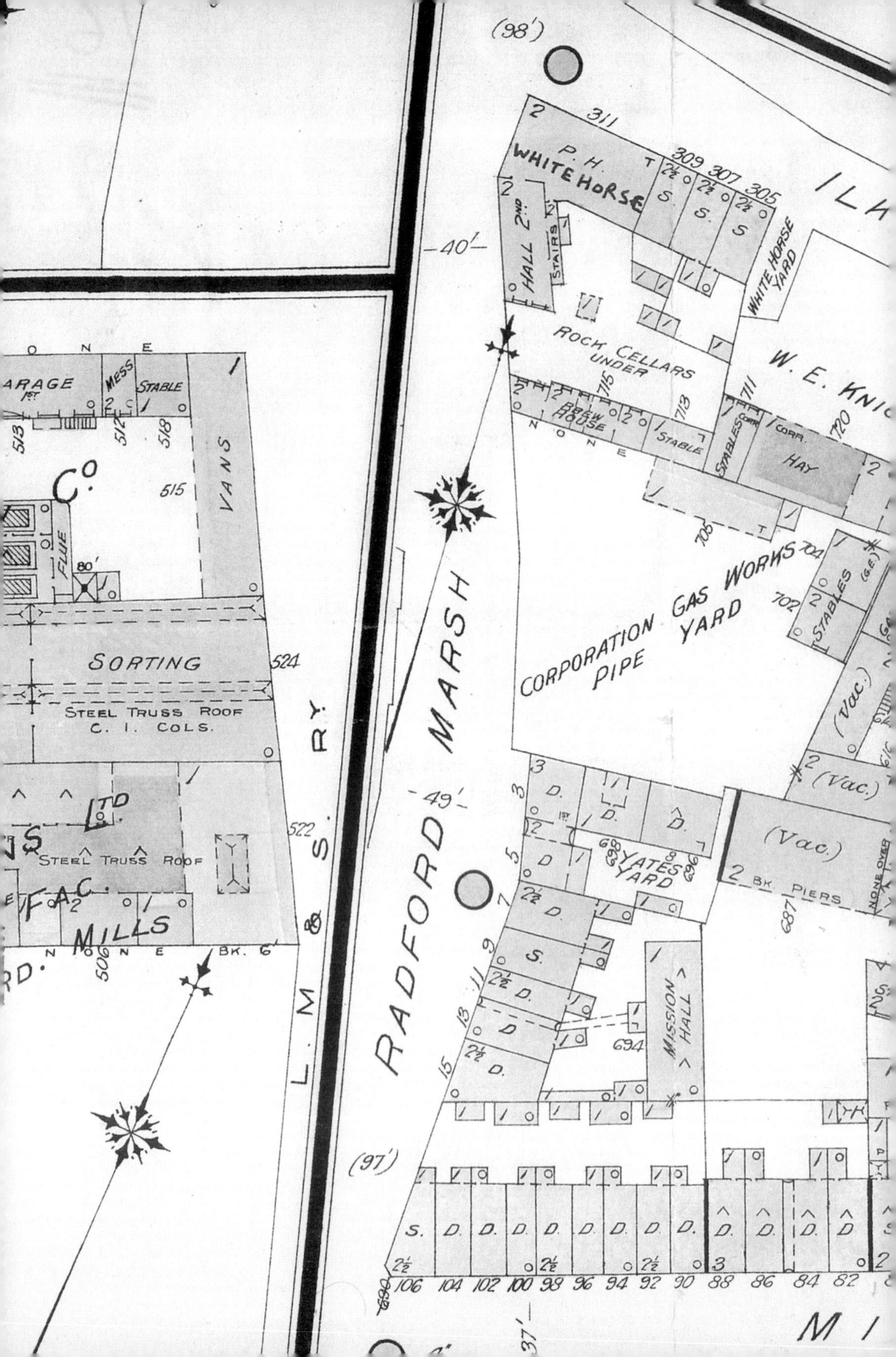

(98')
P. H.
WHITE HORSE
309 307 305
WHITE HORSE YARD
HALL 2ND
STAIRS
ROCK CELLARS UNDER
W. E. KNI
BREW HOUSE
STABLE
STABLES
HAY
CORPORATION GAS WORKS PIPE YARD
STABLES
(Vac.)
YATES YARD
2 BK. PIERS
MISSION HALL
RADFORD MARSH
L. M. & S. RY.
SORTING
STEEL TRUSS ROOF
C. I. COLS.
STEEL TRUSS ROOF
MILLS
ARAGE
MESS
STABLE
VANS
FLUE
CO
LTD
(97')
106 104 102 100 98 96 94 92 90 88 86 84 82
MI

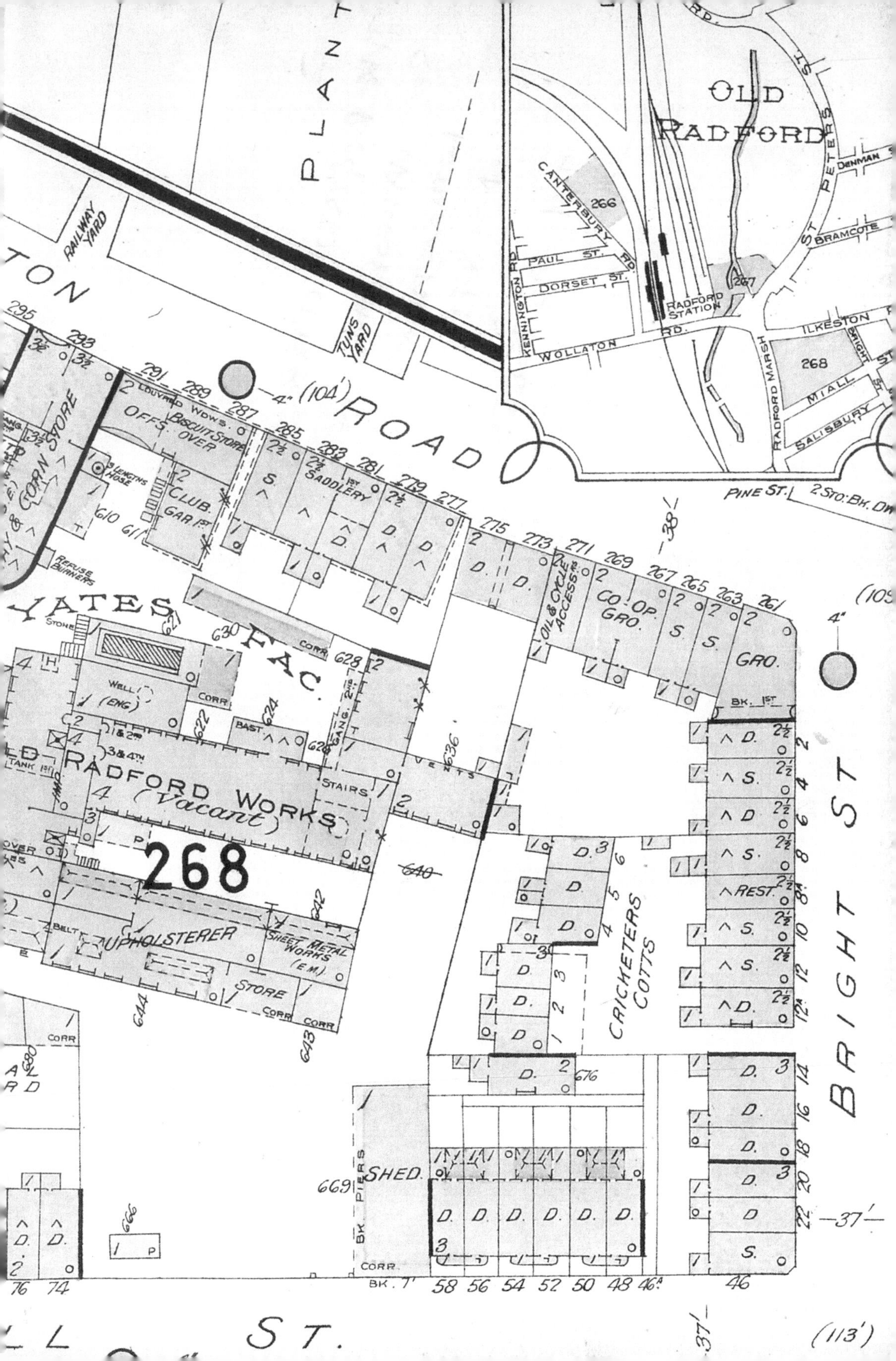

OLD RADFORD
CANTERBURY RD
PAUL ST.
DORSET ST.
KENNINGTON RD
WOLLATON RD.
RADFORD STATION
ST PETERS ST
DENMAN
BRAMCOTE
ILKESTON
RADFORD MARSH
MIALL
SALISBURY
BRIGHT
266
267
268
PINE ST.
2 STO: BK. DW
PLANT
RAILWAY YARD
TUNS YARD
TON
ROAD
YATES FAC.
CORN STORE
BISCUIT STORE
OFFS. OVER
LOUVRED WDWS.
CLUB. GAR 1ST
SADDLERY
OIL & CYCLE ACCESS.
CO-OP. GRO.
GRO.
REFUSE BURNERS
3 LENGTHS HOSE
RADFORD WORKS
4 (Vacant)
268
UPHOLSTERER
SHEET METAL WORKS (E.M.)
STORE
CRICKETERS COTTS
BRIGHT ST
SHED.
BK. PIERS
BK. 7'
ST.
(104')
(113')

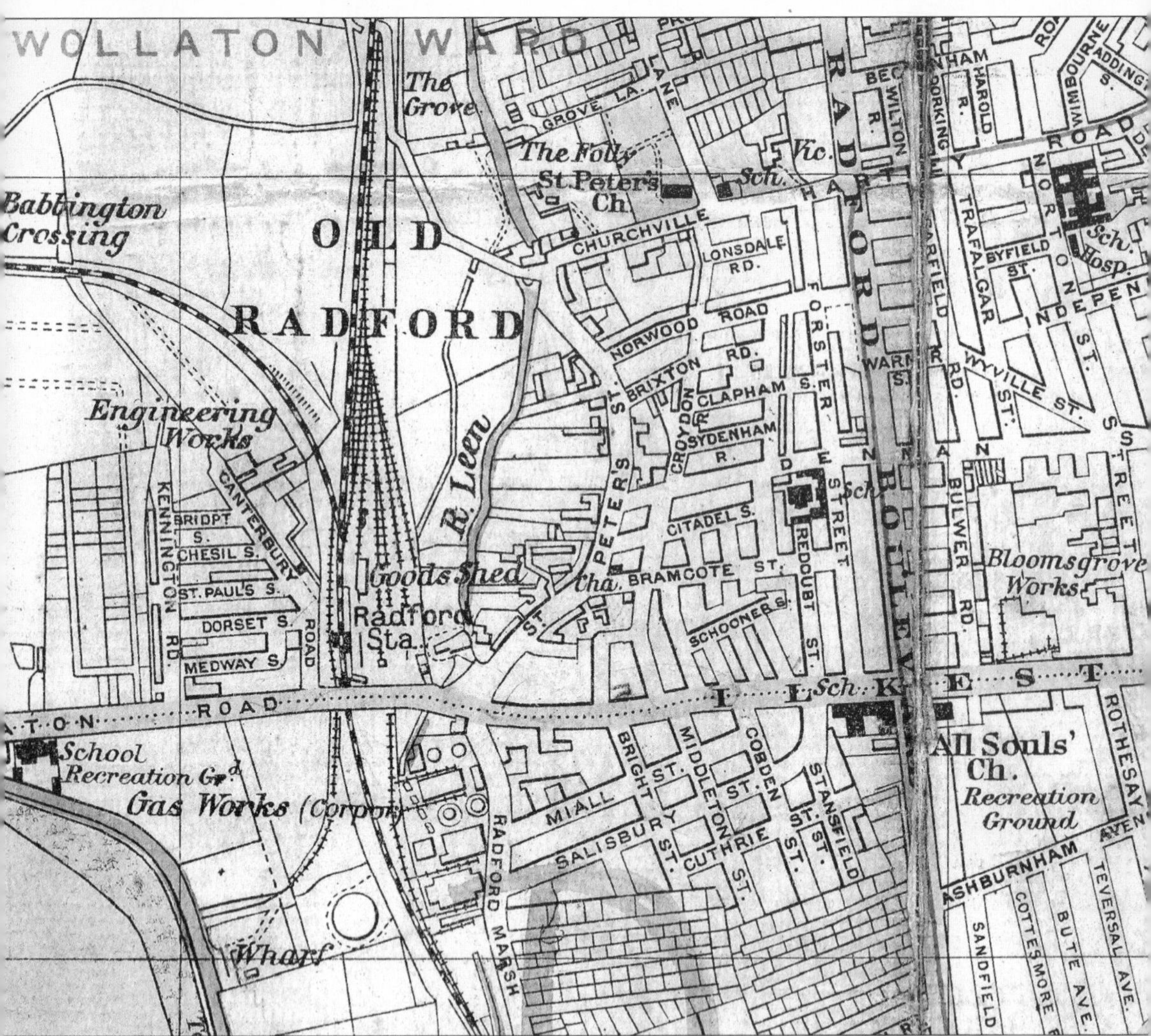

Map of the Radford area, 1908. Radford railway station was opened in 1848 and was served by the Midland Railway and later British Rail until its closure in 1969. Radford Colliery was sunk in 1898, and in the 1950s employed over 1,200 colliers before it closed in 1963. The Raleigh Cycle Company only occupied one side of Radford Marsh at this time, the other side being occupied by a flour mill, canal wharf and Radford Gasworks.

Previous page: Plan of the Ilkeston Road area, 1928. The White Horse Inn, seen at the top left here, had its own brewhouse and stables, confirming that it was once a coaching inn. Most of the buildings on Miall Street were demolished in 1978. Faraday Road is here represented as 'Radford Marsh', the site on which Radford Gasworks was erected in 1844.

Dennis and Anne Hall, 18 Pine Street, 1964. Most of Pine Street was built in 1883, and included the Primitive Methodist chapel, opened in 1830, which later became a motor repair shop. Old Duke Street, Hague Street, Prince Street and Baron Street, as well as the nautically named Schooner and Charter Streets, were cleared in 1965.

GLOVERS (Oil and Grease) Ltd.

OILS, GREASE, SOAP & DISINFECTANT MANUFACTURERS

Suppliers to: Industrial Concerns, Ministries, Schools, Councils, Health Services, etc. We invite your enquiries respecting:—

"MUTAX" — *"GLOSOPOL"* — *"GELOTEX"*

Spotting Fluid • Liquid Detergent • Antiseptic Hand Jelly

LUBRICANTS, LIQUID TOILET and SOFT SOAPS, PINE and CARBOLIC DISINFECTANTS

Ask for full details and samples

Offices: **98-100 St. Peter's Street, Radford, Nottingham**

TELEPHONE: NOTTINGHAM 75579 TELEGRAMS: NOTTINGHAM 75579

Advert for Glover's Oil and Grease Company, 1955. This company was situated at the St Peter's Street/Ilkeston Road junction, opposite Bridge Square, before it was demolished in the early 1970s. Glover's had formerly been known as Cooke and Glover.

VE Day celebrations in St Paul's Street, Radford, in 1945. After six years at war, the time to celebrate had arrived. Today, only the terraced houses on the left-hand side remain on this street, situated just off Kennington Road. Family names from this street in 1945 included: Tuckwood, Kinlock, Hirst, Whyley, Dodsley, Duffy, Hallam, Astill, Boseley, Barnes and Taylor.

Two
Schooldays

Entrance to Alfreton Road School, 1995. This fine example of the stonemason's art was carved in 1880, when this school was built at the Bentinck Road junction. Nine years later, St Michael's and All Angels' church was built directly opposite, but was pulled down in 1975, to make way for a telephone exchange.

City of Nottingham Education Committee.

CITY OF NOTTINGHAM
FORSTER STREET
JUNIOR BOYS' SCHOOL
EDUCATION COMMITTEE

SCHOOL.

DEPARTMENT.

July 24th 1934

Terminal Report of Albert Richards

Class 4

General Work and Conduct during the Term Habitually neat & tidy. Always does excellent work.

Examination Results:

SUBJECT.	POSSIBLE MARKS.	MARKS OBTAINED.
English (including Reading and Composition)	50	42
Arithmetic	50	43

Number in Class 43 *Position in Class* 8th

Remarks: Has greatly improved during year.

Number of Times School opened 134

Times Absent —

Signed A Booth *Class Teacher.*

F. C. Smith *Head Teacher.*

A school report on a pupil at Forster Street Junior Mixed School, 1934. The official school stamp is legible at the top, as is the copperplate script of the master. Left-handed writers would have their fingers rapped with the strap, and one unfortunate boy named Withers, in this class, was often taunted by the teacher with a shout of: 'Are you with us, Withers?' The illiterate adult was not uncommon at this time in a poor area such as Radford.

Norton Street high-rise car park, 1979. Although this derelict car park offered an impressive view of the demolition of the Independent Street area (see p. 87) it was soon transformed into a teenage playground, splashed with graffiti, and was eventually demolished in the mid-1980s. Coal dealers seemed to be the predominant business on Independent Street in 1881, as there were three: Matthew Southern, John Wall and George Garratt. Leroy Wallace Avenue now stands on the site of this car park.

Denman Street, 1981. In the foreground is a house attached to Forster Street School, renamed Sir Sidney Pearson Hill School in 1963, after a famous councillor. It opened in 1877, cost £10,000 to build, and was closed in 1980, when the headmaster was Mr Aslin.

Forster Street School Pageant for VE Day, 1945. Each pupil here is dressed in a costume that was connected with the British Empire. The pupils are seen here at the end of the school day. Resources were few during the war years, with everything being in short supply. Air-raid shelters were sunk into the pavements, although many residents' cellars were strengthened with metal supports for those preferring to stay in their own homes. One of the strangest sights in Radford after the Second World War must have been people queuing for wallpaper at Clarence Walker's shop at 231 Denman Street.

A plaque on Lenton/Radford Library, 1993. The inscription at ground level states that the building was opened in 1925, the stone being laid by Alderman C. Foulds, Chairman of the Public Libraries Committee, on 6 October of that year.

Maun Avenue, 1982. School holidays often provide a time for leisure and fun. Here Simon Archer (hands raised), Julian Bright (centre) and friends play in some old tyre inner tubes by the banks of the River Leen.

Robert Shaw School, Southfield Road, 1971. From left to right, back row: Martin Lombardi, Kevin Pole, -?-, Chris Richards, Robert Langton, Renato Borgazani, Anthony Arnold, Carl Leonard, Andrew Todd, Michael Burchall, Darren Bradley, Mr Severn. Middle row: Tony Bicknall, -?-, Linda Jones, Julia Dring, -?-, Ann Silvers, Helen Swift, Jill Watson, Deborah Mason, Susan Parker, Derek Cousins, Richard Smyth. Front row: Paul Diggle, Andrew ?, Adrian Kelly, Anne Wood, -?-, Cheryl Danby, Elaine Lewis, Andrew Curtis, Michael Bates, Gian Uberti.

Radford Boulevard School, 1998. On Thursday 9 March 1939 there was a prize-giving at All Souls' church where the following girls from this school were presented with prizes: Alice Radford, Madge Richards, Mary Hooley, Beryl Gee, Iris Gee, Joyce Bostock, Lily Badder, Joyce White, Edna Yorke and Marjorie Smith. The school steeple was removed as the Second World War beckoned, as it was considered a navigation aid for enemy aircraft. The bricked-up shop at the Redoubt Street junction was formerly the beer retailer Mary Naylor's shop.

Alfreton Road School inscription, 1990. This school was also known as the Bentinck Road School, and its building plans were submitted on 31 October 1879. In 1889, the teachers at the school would have included Miss Kendal and Miss Louise Penny.

Playground in Forster Street, 1982. The three-storey terraced houses of Forster Street are here part-hidden by the playground. In 1890, an irate father fired a pistol through the front door of Forster Street School, but fortunately there were no casualties.

Three

John Player & Sons

John Player No. 3 Factory by night, 1983. This impressive illuminated sign could be seen from many miles away, but was taken down in 1987 (see p. 37). This view was photographed from Ainsley Road.

NOTTINGHAM DISTRICT

A.D.M. VENUE CHOSEN

WHEN, on December 11, the district committee met for the fifth time since its formation, it learned that membership had been well maintained up to the end of the September quarter, when the figure was 4,012. A steady increase in the Union's strength had taken place since the re-organisation in the district.

The secretary, Jack Griffin, also reported that TOBACCO WORKER sales were rising steadily, and that our monthly quota had been raised to a thousand. He anticipated that even this figure would soon be exceeded. Support for the tobacco tax campaign was still increasing and Chesterfield was the latest Trades Council to signify its backing. Nottingham area of the E.T.U. was with us in the campaign, various branches of the Painters' Union had collected signatures to the petition, and our own Leicester branch had so far sent in 8 completed forms. The district social secretary announced that the social committee would be unable to make any grants at Christmas to superannuated, sick and unemployed members owing to the loss on the dance on November 26.

A special A.D.M. arrangements committee—**Miss Cecil,** and **Bros. Bayliss, Betts, Straw, Wood** and **Wootton**—was charged with the responsibility of securing a venue for the annual conference.

It has since been decided that the A.D.M. will take place in the Albert Hall Institute, Derby Road, Nottingham. This venue was chosen after the district organiser had inspected some 30 prospective places. It is hoped to introduce a number of innovations which will contribute to the smooth conduct of the business.

SICK SOCIETY.—For some years there has been in existence a society known as *The Nottingham T.W.U. Sick Society*. It is conducted by Union members employed at Player's, and membership of the Union is a condition of society membership. It is now seeking to extend, and welcomes male members from all departments. Contributions are 1s. per week, and benefits 25s. per week for the first 12 weeks and 12s. 6d. per week for a further 12 weeks. Members are entitled to benefit after 13 weeks' contributions have been paid. The secretary is **"Bill" Elliott,** and he works in the No. 2 Cutting Dept. of Player's No. 1 Factory.

Frank Swinscoe (Nottingham No. 3) and his wife, snapped at a Union dance. He is a leading light on the social side.

UNION PLAYS SANTA CLAUS.—At the suggestion of **Jim Barnes,** Nottingham members helped to brighten Christmas for the children at the City of Nottingham Children's Homes by purchasing toys. The district committee contributed £5, and No. 5 Branch raised a further £12 5s.

THEATRICAL ENTERPRISES TOO!—On January 7, the district social committee "bought the house" at the People's Theatre where "Dick Whittington" was on the bill. The show was greatly enjoyed, **the majority of the audience being children from schools in the neighbourhood of Player's Factory,** who were given tickets at reduced prices. There were also 14 children from the City of Nottingham Children's Homes. The cast consisted entirely of members of the Drama Group of the Co-operative Arts Centre, and it was their first venture into this field of entertainment. Some of us are still singing "*I Want a Nice Hot Water Bottle.*" (continued on page 17)

Excerpt from *The Tobacco Worker*, 1949. Joyce and Frank Swinscoe are the couple featured in the picture. Frank worked firstly in the cutting room, and then as an electrician, while Joyce was a packer at the No. 2 factory. Fellow packers in the late 1950s would have included Edna Henrys, Edith Mathews and Ivy Cresswell.

Cigarette advertisement, 1945. Advertising manager George Green, who retired in 1945 after fifty years' service, coined the slogan 'Player's Please'. Retailers Salmon & Cluckstein ensured the constant supply of cigarettes to tobacconists' shops.

Bond Cottage and Bonded Imperial Tobacco Warehouses, Triumph Road, 1992. Built in 1939, these warehouses had a capacity of 20,000 tons of leaf tobacco, the tallest being nine storeys high, containing 4 million bricks. These impressive buildings are still standing today.

Player's Factory entrance, 1982. This ornate gateway was situated halfway up Beckenham Road, on the left-hand side, opposite Harold Road, and it is said that in the 1930s men would patiently queue here for work. It was sadly destroyed during the factory's demolition in 1986. In the 1950s, local businesses would have included Bertha Boff, shopkeeper, at 61 Beckenham Road, and at No. 63 Walter Jones' Dining Rooms, directly opposite this gate. This section of the Player works was known as the Castle Tobacco Factory.

Date plaque on Castle Cavendish Works, Dorking Road, 1989. Known as the Player's No. 4 factory, this was a cardboard and sample store from 1903, becoming the Castle Cavendish Works in 1914. In the Second World War, shell parts were produced here. This plaque seems to have survived both wars unscathed.

Castle Cavendish Works, 1999. This factory ceased its John Player association in 1983, when Rex Carnall locked the doors for the last time. It was then the engineer's office. The plaque in the picture above is located just to the right of the arched doorway.

Beckenham Road, 1981. This early morning shot shows the street now known as Norton Street, as the original road seen in the distance has been blocked off. The building on the right foreground is the Player's No. 4 factory, also called the Castle Cavendish Works. Also, branching off to the right are Harold Road and Wilton Street. This area also enclosed Crewe Terrace and Stilton Terrace, cleared in 1979.

Advertisement for Player's cigarettes, 1945. The famous Players sailor featured here was Thomas Huntley Wood, who was photographed in 1897 while serving on the warship *Edinburgh*. The John Player trademark of a sailor's head, two ships and a lifebuoy was patented in 1891.

Dismantling the No. 3 factory roof, January 1987. Each day, one more letter would disappear; the giant fans for the factory's cooling system are exposed here by demolition. The snow-covered rooftops in the distance are on Churchfield Lane.

John Player's Factory Workers, 1980. Here, workers pass the No. 2 factory on Hartley Road after finishing their shift. In the 1940s, Player's girls wore different colour lapels to designate their department: Player's Angels – blue, Leaf Department – brown, Despatch – red and Fancy Department – lavender. 1980 saw the release of John Player Special cigarettes, in black and gold packs, priced at 67p for twenty.

Harold Road, 1978. Ben, Oliver, Lawrence, Grant and Graham Streets are part of a group of Radford streets that were given male Christian names. The shops to the left and right were before closure a café and a pawnbroker's formerly owned by Joe Moore.

Hartley Road, 1981. The Boulevard Works on the right dominates this early morning view. The John Player No. 2 factory rises up on the left. John Player purchased this tobacco business in 1877 but after his death in 1884, his two sons John and William Player took over, soon establishing this Radford industry. The Medium Navy Cut cigarette was introduced in 1900, by which time the business employed 1,000 workers. In 1906, Player's Navy Mixture loose tobacco would have cost 4d per ounce and the brands produced would have included Tawny Navy Cut, Airman Flake and Digger Shag.

John Player No. 2 factory, 1987. This factory was built in 1931 by William Woodsend of Castle Boulevard and had a floor space of 220,000 square feet. Here, the impressive entrance and exit gates of this factory can be clearly seen.

Hartley Road, 1981. On the immediate left is the Player's packing case factory. This was demolished in 1987, along with the Player's No. 2 and No. 3 factories. The building with the pointed roof is St Peter's church hall, formerly the site of the Chequers alehouse.

Player's Works seen from Harold Road, 1980. This devastated back yard is dwarfed by the John Player No. 2 factory rising up behind it, which initially in the 1930s was used solely for Medium Navy Cut cigarette production. This cigarette got its name from the sailors' custom of storing pressed tobacco in a coil of rope, unwinding it as and when needed, to reveal the plug of pressed leaf. The rear of the Windsor Cinema is also visible in this photograph. This picture house was built on the site of a former chapel. It opened in 1939 and closed in 1963, when the entrance fee would have been just over 2s.

Hartley Road, 1983. The site of the Tobacco Workers Union office is situated just under the white canopy. Just past Draper's gun shop is the old Windsor Cinema, which was then the showroom for Player's No. 6 cigarette gifts, where coupons could be exchanged for goods. The showroom was on Player Street from 1967 to 1972, when it moved here to Hartley Road. The old cinema building now houses a carpet warehouse.

Demolition of No. 1 factory, 2000. Ron Thorne started work here in 1941 and received 15s for his first week's work. The despatch department was also based here. In 1976, John Player's No. 6 and No. 10 brands accounted for half of all British cigarette sales.

Four

Raleigh Industries

Raleigh Gate 4, 1998. Situated on Faraday Road almost directly opposite Salisbury Street, this entrance was pulled down in August 2000. In the early 1970s, school leavers would be interviewed in a room just inside the gate. A qualified spot welder at this time would hope to earn £20 per week.

Lisa Richards and Brian Sillitoe, Raleigh Athletic Club, 1950s. Although the Athletic Club on Old Coach Road was situated at Wollaton, it was still within walking distance for the Raleigh employee. Built in 1930 and demolished in 1986, the Club offered a 34-acre sports ground, with bowls, tennis, archery, cricket, tennis and football facilities. There was also a fishing lake. Brian, the younger brother of Radford writer Alan Sillitoe, is seen here during a break from his National Service. The steward at this time was Mr Waldron. A new housing development now stands on the site of the Athletic Club.

Colin Lee (left) and friend, 1974. Around the time this photograph was taken, a Raleigh employee would hope to earn about £30 per week. In 1966, a West Indian Raleigh worker met a young musician named Jimi Hendrix in a Nottingham club, who, it is said, was given overnight accommodation at his house on Faraday Road, Radford.

Raleigh factory, Faraday Road, 2000. This wall seems to be the Raleigh worker's approximation of a telephone book, although the telephone itself has long since been removed. This vast factory had many departments and extensions, employing over 9,000 workers in the 1960s.

Madge Russ, Brian Sillitoe and Lisa Richards on a Raleigh trip to Blackpool, 1954. Raleigh organized annual outings to popular resorts; this one departed from Victoria railway station. These trips were well documented in the firm's glossy *Raligram* magazine, which cost 3d in 1956 and described the factory as 'The world's largest and most modern cycle plant'. In 1952, a Raleigh Sports cycle could be acquired for £16.

The Bachelors visit Raleigh, 1964. This Irish trio, consisting of brothers Conleth and Declan Clusky and John Stokes, had just had a No. 1 hit with 'Diane' when they made this visit. In 1982, Liverpool group The Merseybeats appeared at the Raleigh Social Club.

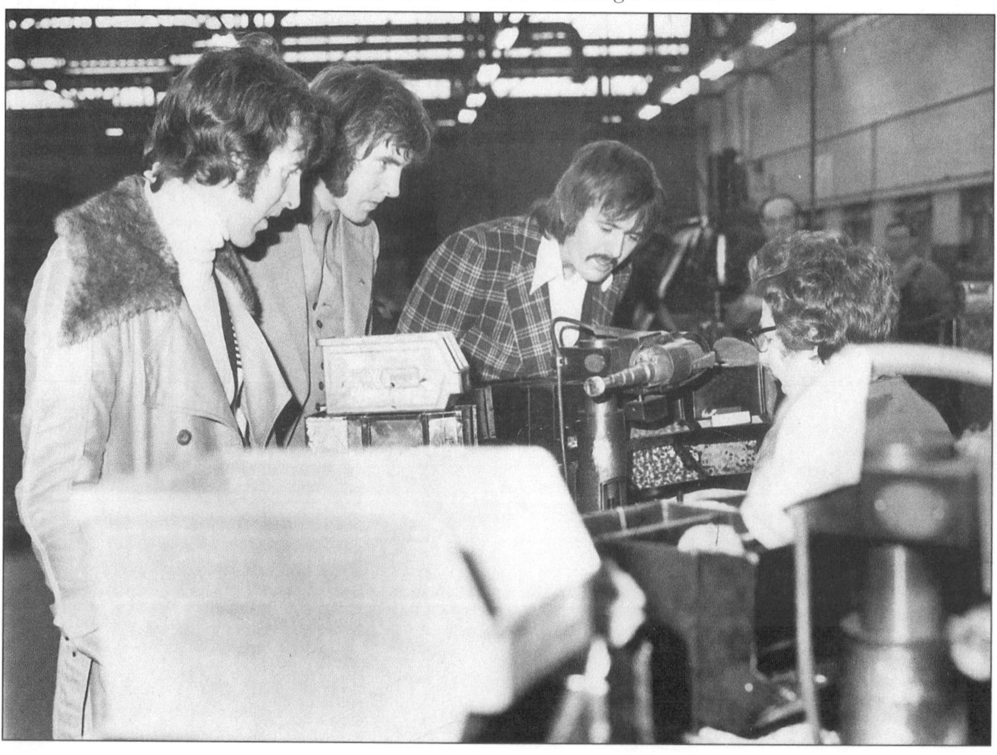

Christmas at Raleigh Ballroom, 1974. The annual employees dinner was held at this building on Lenton Boulevard, built in 1931, which had a frontage of 350ft. The architect was F.C. Howitt, who designed the famous Nottingham Council House. The first floor had a showroom for Raleigh products, a dining room and a concert hall, where many famous bandleaders such as Joe Loss played. My parents Harry and Lisa Richards are on the left of the picture. Frank and Marlene Gee and her sister Joy are sitting on the right. This building has now been renamed the Marcus Garvey Centre.

THE RALEIGH SOCIAL CLUB

Membership Card—1981

Expires 31 December, 1981

1. This card is not transferable.
2. This card to be shown on request to the Manager or any other Raleigh Social Club Official.
3. Two visitors per day but one visitor not more than 12 times per year may be signed in by a member on payment of 20p.
4. Visitors may not purchase drinks.
5. The Management reserves the right to refuse admission.

Raleigh Social Club pass, 1981. Each employee was given free membership to the Social and Athletic Clubs. The manager of the club in the 1970s was a Scot named John Faye. Home Ales Bitter in 1981 cost the princely sum of 33p a pint.

The Social Club shortly before demolition, August 2000. This was founded in 1972 from the former Works Canteen. The social club had 2,000 members by 1984 when, under protest, it was closed down and computer equipment installed in the building. This club, in its day, offered a separate snooker room with full-size tables, playing host to celebrities such as Alex Higgins and Dennis Taylor in the early 1980s.

Raleigh Offices, Lenton Boulevard, 1979. Administration at Raleigh was just as important as bicycle production; the substantial filing clerks' department is shown here. In 1980, Raleigh introduced the Shopper cycle, at a price of £110, followed in 1981 by the Hercules Folda, with a collapsible U-frame, costing £70. In 1983, the BMX Burner was launched. Bicycle designs were tested with a piece of sophisticated equipment called 'Cardboard Fred', a puppet made of card, which had jointed arms and legs and tested the ergonomic properties of the cycle prototypes.

Harry Richards at the bench grinder in the Parkerising department, 1978. In this year, solar panels were fitted on the roof of the Faraday Road factory to heat the water in the boiler house. Even in the 1970s, however, the traditional methods of bicycle production were being increasingly replaced by automation.

Raleigh No. 3 factory, Wollaton Road, 1985. Completed in August 1957, this £5 million factory was 1,690ft long and contained 4,000 tons of steel. Apprentices who started at Raleigh in 1959 included toolmakers M. Colbert, M. Wells and D. Plant.

Demolition of the Faraday Road factory, 1990. In its heyday, Raleigh produced such classic cycles as the Blue Streak and Pink Witch in 1958, and the Lenton Marque III and Triumph Jack of Clubs. The Pink Witch with its shocking lipstick-coloured finish and vanity mirror was aimed purely at the teenage girl. The sporty Blue Streak model boasted a brilliant silver finish with metallic blue trimmings.

Bridge Clock, Faraday Road, 1987. Built to link one side of the Raleigh factory on Faraday Road to the other, this bridge was completed in April 1952. The clock hands are here frozen at twelve o'clock, as the power had by now been disconnected. It was sturdily constructed, with four mechanical conveyors carrying cycle parts across the road, to be assembled and packed on the other side. By the mid-1980s, however, this bridge had been dismantled.

Sturmey Archer gear factory, Cycle Road, 1990. This 410-foot long factory was opened in 1922, and offered a floor space of 33,000 square feet. It was mainly employed in the manufacture and testing of three-speed hub assemblies. In 1922, over 2,000 people were employed at Raleigh.

The roof of the Faraday Road factory, 1990. Raleigh acquired many famous names in its chequered history. In 1932 it bought Humber cycles, and Rudge in 1938. Triumph followed in 1954, with BSA and Sunbeam being absorbed in 1957.

Chris Richards at Raleigh Athletic Club, 1972. The vastness of the club's cricket field is apparent here. The licensees at this time were Leslie and Irene Eley. One of the star Raleigh team cricketers at this time was Geoff Tokelove. The last licensee in 1986 was Alan Beaumont.

Demolition of the Turnery Department, Faraday Road, 1990. This section of buildings was used to film the famous opening sequence in Alan Sillitoe's *Saturday Night and Sunday Morning*. Times in nearby Ward's Yard and Beaconsfield Terrace must have been noisy ones, especially during a night shift at the factory.

Salisbury Street Cycle Mural, 1989. This mural once depicted Raleigh cycles from past to present, but has since been reduced to a low wall. The centre of this picture was the approximate site of 5 Beaconsfield Terrace, former home of famous local author Alan Sillitoe. Actor Albert Finney stayed in this house during the making of *Saturday Night and Sunday Morning* in 1959, and was taken into the nearby Marquis of Lorne pub to polish up his Nottingham accent for the film. Most of Salisbury Street disappeared in the late 1970s, and now houses mainly small industrial units.

A sign on Faraday Road, 1988. The speed at which cycle production increased after the First World War is impressive. In 1911, 50,000 cycles had been made, but the figure for 1946 had risen to 400,000, and to 750,000 by 1949. By 1951, bicycle production had topped a million units. Raleigh Industries will always be known to Radford people simply as 'The Raleigh', and many sons followed fathers and even grandfathers into this workplace.

Gate 9, Faraday Road, 1989. The Faraday Road factories were so vast that more than one entrance gate had to be provided. At the end of a shift, a sea of workers, on foot and also on bicycles, would swarm down Faraday Road, all dressed in the regulation blue overalls.

Fire station gates, Faraday Road, 1990. In April, 1969, there was a fire in the enamelling shop of the Faraday Road factory. Prior to this, an arson attempt had been made on the old Ilkeston Road Picture House in June 1963.

The Faraday Road factory, summer 1990. A fine example of old sign-writing, but somewhat marred by the vandals' attacks on the factory windows. This five-acre factory stretched all the way from Salisbury Street to Johnson Road.

Raleigh office buildings, Faraday Road, 1990. These offices were erected next to Gate 9 in 1921. Sadly, Frank Bowden, who founded the Raleigh Cycle Company in 1888, died in that year. 1921 saw a record 100,000 cycles produced, which surpassed the previous record of 60,000, set in 1914.

Four

Streets

An alleyway off Lonsdale Road, 1982. A familiar sight in Radford, this particular entry still connects Hartley Road with Lonsdale Road. Just behind the wall on the right is a building, formerly FFG Hosiery Ltd, makers of silk hosiery, but now a printing works.

The Boulevard Hotel, Radford Boulevard, 1981. This popular public house was named after the road on which it stands. The small shops on the left are the former businesses of Whittle's confectioners and Mary Wright's chip shop. Edith Terrace was located behind this building, until its destruction in 1980. The licensee of the hotel in 1888 was Frederick Dale. This pub now enjoys the student custom of the nearby Norton Court hall of residence.

Waterloo Promenade, Forest Road West, 1927. These houses have long since been replaced with industrial units. The Windley School is situated on Waterloo Promenade, which connects Alfreton Road with the Forest. A more recent shot of these impressive gateposts can be seen on p. 110.

R.C. Keetch, engineers, 1998. This building on Bramcote Street survived the 1965 demolition programme and is still in use today. The entrance to Gatling Street is on the far left, and Bastion Street is to the right.

Dawn breaking, Hartley Road, 1982. The Colonel Burnaby public house on the right changed its name to the Penny Farthing in that year, but reverted to the old name in 1986. The road to the left of the pub is Denison Street, which contained Alice Hough's ice cream makers and William Lilley's chip shop in the 1950s. The Regal Social Club and The Salvation Army barracks were also situated on this street, as was Fryma Fabrics. In the early twentieth century the Radford and District Liberal Club and the Old Farm House Inn would also have been found here. Former landlady Ivy Flower was licensee of the Colonel Burnaby for over twenty-five years.

A café on Boden Street, 1982. A special feature here is the rounded brickwork end to the shop. The Round House at 106 Denman Street (demolished in 1966) shared this architectural feature. The wall on the right belongs to the Radford Baths and Laundry, now a garage.

Ilkeston Road, 1982. The White Horse public house is on the right, while the newer houses to the left are on the old plot of the Three Tuns alehouse, which was situated between Tuns Yard and Railway Yard, demolished in the early twentieth century.

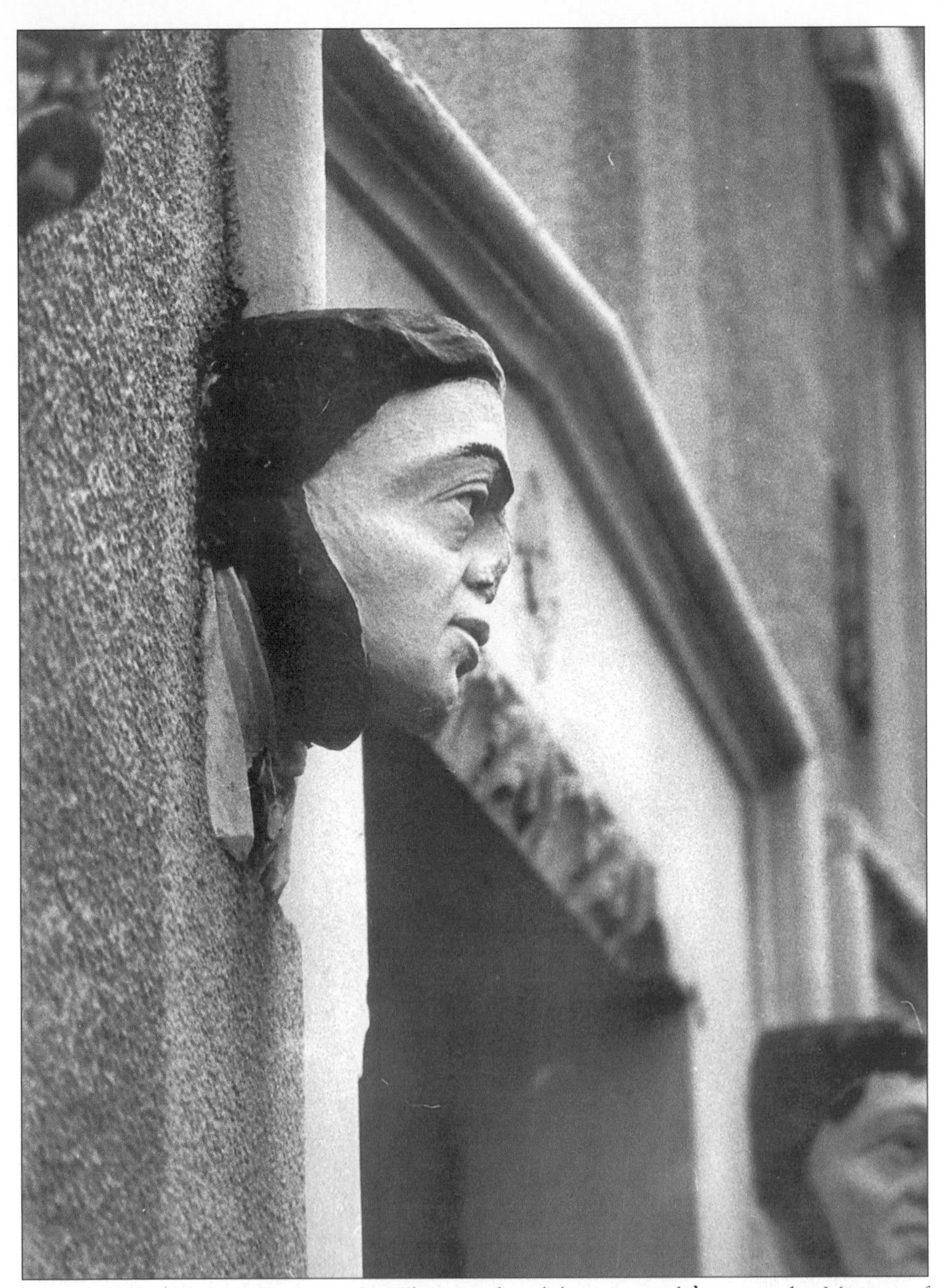

Variety Club, Salisbury Street, 1981. This popular club is situated opposite the Marquis of Lorne public house, and has been here since at least the early 1970s. This building was untouched by the demolition work of 1978 that claimed most of this street. Shops that disappeared included: John Pendleton, beer retailer, Florence Hind, grocer and Harvey Rhodes' fried fish shop. Miniature versions of these stone gargoyles are also present above the windows of the Dover Castle public house on Denman Street.

Skill's Motor Coaches, St Peter's Street, 1998. This business was founded in 1919 by Arthur Skill, and is still managed by his grandchildren, Simon and Nigel. It was built on land by the River Leen, formerly occupied by Rudkins and White, sawmill owners and wheelwrights.

St Peter's church, Hartley Road, 1993. This was the first church to be erected in Radford. It was rebuilt from a ruin in 1812 at a cost of £2,000, when fragments of an eleventh-century church wall were discovered while digging out the foundations.

Denman Street, 1979. The rag and bone man, or 'tatter' as he is known to Radford people, is passing the Denman Furnishing Stores on Bulwer Road. Often a horse and cart was used by these men, whose ghostly cry of 'rag-bone' could be heard from several streets away.

Demolition on Rifle Street, 1980. A rather wet Dover Castle pub stands in the centre, with the van and shop belonging to Henry and Edith Cooper of 26 Citadel Street. The public house here still sports its original red Shipstones Ales lettering.

Forster Street, 1982. A fine example of the rather better quality Denman Street shop, with elaborate bay windows above. The shop on the left, now a derelict bookmaker's shop, was a century ago William Fryer's fishmongers. The café was a butcher's shop from the early 1900s onwards, passing to G.J. Banks, pork butcher, in 1904. Two small terraces, Forster Grove and Forster Avenue, were demolished in the clearance programme of 1980. The brickwork tower of the Forster Street school, which was directly opposite, was deemed unstable in 1937 and promptly dismantled.

Radford Baths and Laundry, Thackerey Street, 1982. This splendid building was opened on 28 June 1880, and cost £5,150 to build. The laundry was added in 1926. Tom Blower, the famous local swimmer, trained here in the 1930s; he swam the English Channel in 1937 in a time of 13 hours 29 minutes, earning him the nickname 'Torpedo Tom'. He was originally a machine mechanic from the John Player tobacco works. Boden Street can be seen at the end of this road, where Franks and Son, funeral directors, and Garratt and Hemphney, coal merchants, traded until the demolition of the street in the mid-1960s.

Denman Street, 1980. Many Radford children spent their summer holidays at a children's playground with swings, roundabout and paddling pool, opposite this junction. Now this street extends only as far as the end of the pub, as a playground and grassed area has been laid. The building on the right is the Dover Castle public house.

Croydon Road, 1980. On the left is Gary Elliott, of Kennington Road. In the 1940s, the Toone's plywood factory next to these houses had 'steaming vats of brown animal glue which looked like liquid toffee but turned the stomach with a foul odour'.

F.G. Shepherd's Motors, New Bridge, 1984. This business still stands on what was part of Radford Folly, a pleasure garden originally built by William Elliot in the 1780s. The surrounding area has been redeveloped into Midland Court, a modern industrial precinct.

Warner Street, 1980. The lady is just about to cross Garfield Road, past the ruin of Edith Butler's off-licence. The deck-access flats in the distance are Connaught Gardens, which along with neighbouring Denman Gardens, were demolished in the 1990s.

Hartley Road, 1984. The large building in the distance is the Marathon Knitwear factory, also known as the Boulevard Works. The street on the far left is Trafalgar Street, demolished in 1980, which also contained Trafalgar Terrace. Hartley Road was formerly Outgang Lane, which connected the old Radford Village with the Forest. It was renamed in 1877 after William Hartley, the famous maker of jams and preserves. Then, the only occupants would have been John Turner, shopkeeper, and the Revd Charles Lea Wilson, vicar of St Peter's church. In the mid-1960s, Krazy Cuts, one of Radford's first mini-markets, was opened at 67 Hartley Road.

Grandmother and grandchild, Forster Street, 1981. One feature of this terraced house is that the guttering at the front is built into the brickwork, as seen by the rain outlet by the lady's feet. This house was situated next to Birkin's lace factory.

Walking up Brixton Road, 1982. Brixton, Norwood, Dulwich and Croydon Road were all named after South London areas. Half a century ago, you may have found shopkeepers Edna Perkins and John Harrison trading there.

Demolition of Bendix Launderette, Hartley Road, 1984. This building has an interesting history. Firstly a wickermaker's, then a confectioner's shop, it passed to the Baumber family between the wars, where first Frances and later Grace kept a grocer's shop. Nos 89-93 Hartley Road are on the right.

The Boulevard Hotel and Grundy Athletic Club, 1982. In the 1940s, this former stable building was a popular boys' boxing club, but was demolished in the 1990s. The advertisement hoarding on the right is advertising an 'Emgas Sale'.

Mother and child on Norton Street, 1980. The lady is walking past the site of 119 Norton Street, where Horace Smith's turf commissioners once stood. Norton Street's main industry was Manlove and Alliot's engineers, who were listed in 1864 as being 'an engineers, sugar washing and drying machine manufacturers'. The firm was established in 1837 and closed in 1972. Wyche and Coppock's boat builders were also based on this street, as was Mr Edward Day, the cane furniture manufacturer. The building to the extreme left is the ruin of 2 Arthur Terrace, off Independent Street.

Radford Boulevard, 1982. Horace Bird's chemist shop is evident here on the left, his son John Bird was later to become an actor. The Pricewise Mini-Market seen opposite was formerly the World Radio Supply Stores but enjoyed a short spell as Marsden's grocers. This supermarket still serves the local community today.

Clearance of Denman Street, 1980. The last opening remaining on the left-hand side is St John's Terrace, home in the 1920s to the Premier Pattern Co. Annfield, Leonard and Plimsoll Terrace were its neighbouring yards. Denman Street was formerly known as St John's Road.

Dulwich Road, 1982. An elderly resident is standing on distant Norwood Road, while children play on old mattresses discarded during demolition. The building on the left is the Nottingham Arms public house, advertising Gold Label beer.

Ortzen Street, 1982. The cleared land to the right was the site of the Marquis of Waterford public house, a Whitbread beer house named after Field Marshal Earl Roberts (1832-1914). In the 1880s the landlord was A. Heggs.

Six

Winter

Car on Burns Street, 1981. In the early 1900s Burns Street was home to many architects and solicitors, as well as Blood's coal merchants and Frederick Goddard's lace factory. Nottingham Education Committee Girls' Hostel was also on this street. The editor of the Nottingham Guardian, Richard Ivens, lived here in the 1920s.

Simmons' hardware shop, Denman Street, 1981. This long-standing Radford business was established in the 1880s, when the Simmons family sold goods from a horse and cart. Frank Simmons took this shop over in 1940 from Abraham Cohen, and started selling china, hardware and household sundries. His son Barry later joined this family business. Frank retired in 1995, after running the shop for fifty-five years. The business was one of the last remaining Denman Street shops, and never lost sight of the two most important shopkeepers' rules: service and traditional values.

Marathon Knitwear factory, Radford Boulevard, 1981. This building, known as the Boulevard Works, was built in 1896 and earlier in the twentieth century housed Martin and Holliwell, lace curtain manufacturers, The Broxtowe Warp Knitting Company, Burt Brothers (Hosiery) and Strong Meakin, silkscreen printers. It is now the home of Bentwood Limited.

Hartley Road, 1981. The woman is walking towards the junction with the Bendix launderette at the corner of Trafalgar Street. The wasteland beyond is the old site of the Nottingham Scattered Children's Home, formerly a workhouse built in 1838, and the Barnett's sweet factory, which by this time had relocated to Cobden Street. This confectioner's, established in 1890 by Richard Barnett, was renowned for its 'energy sweets' – Lun Jeelers, Fruit Drops and Sherbons – as well as its Barley Sugar and Mirror Mints. The large block of flats is Bampton Court, which collectively with Buckland, Bladon and Broadway Court, were known as the 'Four Bs'.

John Player tobacco factory, Beckenham Road, 1981. Built in 1884, this factory was used for lace manufacture before turning over to tobacco production in the early 1900s. It was demolished in the 1990s and the site now houses Norton Court students' hall of residence.

Shopping in the snow, Denman Street area, 1981. These ladies are walking across the approximate site of Wyville Street. Weeds have already started breaking through the cleared land beyond. Garfield Road is the street visible in the distance.

Denman Street, 1981. Looking down towards St Peter's Street, the land on the right hand side had been the site of Anderson's pawnshop, Cheetham's Stores and Jim Jones' men's hairdressers at 316 Denman Street. This barber's shop was famous for its well-worn burgundy leather chairs and the picture of the 1959 Nottingham Forest FA Cup-winning team in the window. Jim would chat about the First World War with the pipe-smoking veterans who came to have a haircut, and such services as a singe, crew-cut or shave would be offered, even in the late 1970s, with the open razor being sharpened on a strap in the corner. The business closed with the demolition of the shop in 1980.

Imperial Tobacco Bonded Warehouses, 1981. The snow-covered gardens of houses on the Ainsley Estate curve round to meet the playing fields for The Robert Shaw Primary School and the smoke from the industries in the Canterbury Road area. In the 1950s, industries in this area included Viking Engineering and the Victoria Laundry and Dyeworks. At the time this picture was taken, John Player tobacco workers at the Bonded Warehouses included: Len Laing, warehouseman; Ken Palmer, chargehand; and Barrie Heath, warehouse manager.

John Player No. 2 factory, Radford Boulevard, 1981. A popular game for local children was to attempt to throw a ball onto the roof of this factory. The old clock from the front of this building now stands on a plinth in the new Retail Park.

Forster Street, 1981. Here, photographed at from the Hartley Road junction, these houses are facing the back of the Boulevard Works. The Methodist chapel at the other end of Forster Street was built in 1890, the contractor being M.W. Savage.

Boy running in the rain, Alfreton Road, 1981. The butchers shop here belongs to L. Wright, while other shops in the area included Sounds Good secondhand records, Cousin's chip shop, Olivia Jude and Three D Shoes. This photograph was taken from the doorway of the Running Horse public house, a premier live music venue even now.

Churchfield Lane, 1981. The wall and trees on the left-hand side are part of St Peter's churchyard, while the John Player's No. 3 and Glebe works dominate the other side. The 150-foot tall boiler house chimney was pulled down in March 1987.

Larkdale Street, 1981. Most of the villas on this street were built in 1875. The first two dwellings with bay windows on the left are former boarding houses, which belonged to Cicely Duthrie in the 1950s. The Methodist Minister, the Revd John Davidson, lived on this street in the 1930s.

Needham's motorcycle shop, Wollaton Road, 1993. This business relocated from Hartley Road in the early 1980s to this former grocer's shop, and is owned by former boxer Dave Needham, who won the British Bantamweight championship in 1974.

Demolition of the Garfield Road area, 1980. This panorama is photographed from Norton Street Car Park, with the John Player No. 2 factory and Boulevard Works visible in the rain. Former occupants of this grim wasteland were: Colton Dairies cheese makers, the Forest Lion alehouse, the United Methodist church, Hudson's motorcycle dealers and Moore & Son, producers of milk and dairy products. Neighbouring Landseer Street, Coleridge Street, Mozart Street and Warner Street also vanished in this year.

Russell Street, 1981. The inscription on the clock in Roman numerals gives the date of construction as 1872. Just to the right is Gamble Street, behind which lay a small cluster of houses called Mellon Terrace. This building was formerly used for warehousing and lace production, but has now been beautifully restored as part of the ongoing Alfreton Road regeneration project.

Seven
Public Houses

A night-time photograph of White Horse public house, 1982. Shipstones Ales of Basford supplied this pub at this time, but earlier in the century the pub brewed its own beer in an outbuilding, which became Radford Boys' Boxing Club in 1969. In 1830 there were fourteen independent brewing houses in Radford.

The Marquis of Lorne pub, 1950s. Here, Ethel Yorke, of 44 Salisbury Street, is sitting between daughters Sheila (left) and Ivy (right). Sheila's husband Ted Smith is on the left. Ethel's husband John Yorke worked as a cobbler in Pine Terrace after the First World War.

The Jolly Higglers pub, 1968. This building's licensee was Nellie Allen when this picture was taken. Len and Muriel (Chubb) Harrison took over in 1969, and were renowned for organizing raffles, outings and parties for the Radford community. Prince Street is the junction on the left.

Christmas at the Jolly Higglers, 1989. Barmaids Debbie and Fiona had no hesitation in posing for me here! Note the twin bitter and mild Shipstones pumps at the front of this picture. 'Higglers' were said to be nineteenth-century coal workers who bought coal up to the surface in baskets.

Jolly Higglers, 1999. Now owned by Greenalls, this alehouse was rebuilt in 1970 and moved back to accommodate the new pub car park. Its hot food prices from 1977 make interesting reading: Baked potatoes – 7p; pork and stuffing rolls – 17p.

Frontage of the Crown Inn, Western Boulevard, 1998. The original pub was built opposite the White Horse Inn on Radford Marsh, but was pulled down in 1935, when this replacement was built in 1930s Art Deco style. Its first licensee was Joseph Lee.

Crown Inn, 1991. A quartet of former Raleigh cycle factory workers are shown here, from left to right: Kevin Pashley, John Wiles, Harry Richards and Denis Crofts. It is now a popular student haunt, being opposite the University Jubilee Campus, built on the former Raleigh site in 1999.

Nottingham Arms, Dulwich Road, 1981. The building in the middle distance is the school building, also seen on p. 25. The truncated steeple of the Radford Boulevard School can also be seen. Brixton Road is the cleared street visible on the right, which was partly demolished in 1980 along with Navarino Terrace. The part-demolished dwellings of Radford often housed hidden treasures, long forgotten, in cellars and attics. Boxes of American comics and German telescopes and helmets dating from the First World War were some items recovered during 1980. The pub has now been taken over by Mansfield Brewery and new housing has been built around it.

Cliff and Jean Brown at the White Horse Inn, 1990. This couple moved from Langley Mill in the late 1980s to run this pub. Next door was P. Theodosi's Greek chip shop and restaurant. This pub is also known locally as the 'White Hoss' or the 'Bobbo'.

Last dance at the Marquis of Lorne, 1989. The interior of this public house has now been knocked through into one giant room, and boasts some magnificent stained glass. The licensee at this time was Andy Cooke.

The White Horse Inn, 1989. Pat and Betty are jiving to the music of 'Rocking Ray' Fletcher, who appeared here every Friday night. '50s devotees would travel from all over Nottingham to see Ray, and their vintage American cars could be seen parked on Faraday Road.

Tiled exterior of the White Horse, 1999. These bottle-green tiles were added to the pub in 1912, as were the engraved windows. Similar tiles can also be seen on the exterior of the Generous Briton pub on Alfreton Road, Radford.

The Dover Castle, Denman Street, 1988. The 1921 rates ledger shows a yearly payment of £180 for this pub, formerly a working men's hotel. This establishment has now been converted into flats. The fenced-off land at the front of this photograph is the former site of the Ideal Laundry Co.

The Old Rose, 1989. Landlady Beryl Webb is on the right of this picture. The Old Rose was supplied by Tennants Rock Ales in the 1950s, whose Queen's Bitter and Dark Mild were relished by this pub's customers.

Pub sign for the Marquis of Lorne, 1985. These white and yellow hexagonal signs were a feature of many Radford pubs, and could be illuminated at night (see p. 104). This pub was named after Marquis John Sutherland Campbell (1845-1920).

The Old Rose, 1995. This building dates from 1832 and was known in 1882 as the Rose Revived Inn. In 1921, the licensee was Mabel Dixon. The street to the right is Deakins Place, where Torcross Cottages were located before their demolition in 1958.

Roy Wakefield at the Penny Farthing public house, Hartley Road, 1985. Roy was a former Raleigh labourer who would entertain us with his tales of National Service from just after the Second World War. Other lively Radford characters included 'Bluey', a man who would walk the streets selling blue buttons and rabbits in the 1940s, and the exuberant Albert Brown, who would parade along Denman Street in the 1950s with an electric blue suit and pink socks and tie (or *vice versa*). Musician Cyril Clarke of Salisbury Street was an entertainer in his spare time, playing the electric organ at many local functions, often sporting full tuxedo, slicked-back hair and bow tie.

Building work at The Boulevard Hotel, 1982. The aptly named 'Gun Room' was the venue for many Country and Western nights, and the folk club upstairs was host to many musicians in the 1980s, including the legendary Martin Carthy. This doorway was bricked up during refurbishment in the 1990s.

'Little Elvis' at the Marquis of Lorne, 1989. This disc jockey (real name Tony Miller) was a Friday night fixture at the aforementioned pub. At least six Radford pubs featured rock and roll music on a Friday night in 1989, and 'Elvis' would even mime to the songs of his hero.

Drinking at The Victoria Inn, 9 Highurst Street, 1950s. From left to right: Tony Slater, Keith Barnett, Stan Fletcher. The landlord at the time was Paul Taylor, who had taken over from Fred Tovey, who was listed as being the licensee in 1941.

The Peacock, Bloomsgrove Street, 1998. This street was originally named because it was built on a flower meadow, although the silence was soon shattered by the erection of a glass and bottling works. This pub's ornithological companion, the Pheasant Inn, resides on Prospect Street.

Agnes Aird at the Colonel Burnaby pub, 1986. Agnes was a lively Scottish lady who had moved to Nottingham from Glasgow in the early 1970s. This pub was named after famous Victorian adventurer Frederick Gustavus Burnaby, who crossed the English Channel by balloon in 1882.

Albion Inn, Gamble Street, 1981. The building in the foreground is part of the Gambles factory, one of many large lace and textile factories in the area. An inn of this name is listed as being here in 1866, when the landlord was Thomas Crowe. In 1894, The Gamble Cycle Company was also located on this street.

Walter and Renee Dobson at the Colonel Burnaby pub, 1987. This couple were the licensees of this pub at this time. Renee was a regular at the Spread Eagle pub on nearby Alfreton Road, which was the favourite alehouse of philosopher Herbert Spencer (1820-1903).

New Year at the White Horse Inn, 1989. In the 1950s, before the jukebox, the piano sing-along was a regular event in the back room in this pub, where Harold, a self-taught honky-tonk pianist, would have been resident on a Saturday night.

The Wheatsheaf, Ilkeston Road, 1998. Situated at Ilkeston Road's junction with Montfort Street, this pub was supplied in the 1920s by George Hooley's brewers next to it. Behind this was Greek Square and De Ligne Street, demolished in 1956.

Alma Inn, Alfreton Road, 1981. A dwelling called The Tiled House was listed as being next to this pub in 1889, where John Cox kept a doctor's surgery. The landlord of the Alma Inn, Lester Riley, won a Greenall's 'Best Kept Cellar' award in 1998.

Marquis of Lorne at night, 1985. This pub is seen here from Middleton Street, which was named after landowner Lord Middleton. The Victorian houses on the top half of this street are still standing today, and include a former bakery, next to No. 14.

Portland Arms, Portland Road, 1988. In the 1930s, The Dolphin pub across the road on Ireton Street, offered 'home brewed ales of the finest quality'. At this time, the Portland House Hostel for Women and the premises of stained glass artist Henry Padmore could be found on this street.

Eight

Plaques, Signs and Features

Radford Boulevard and Norwood Road junction, 1985. The impressive brickwork of the Boulevard Works is displayed here in the sunshine. This is one of the last great remaining Radford factories.

Hartley Road sign, 1982. 'Churchville' gained its name because of the close presence of St Peter's church, an early Radford landmark. In the 1930s, there was a ruin of a mill building behind this sign, known to the local children as the Haunted House.

No. 120 Hartley Road, 1982. This shop was formerly a doctor's surgery. Dr Sophia and Dr Keith Stuart are listed as residing here in 1956, but this shop had originally been Thomas Thorpe's fine china shop, in the early 1920s.

Alton's cigar factory, 1995. Edmund Alton founded this business in 1862, but these premises on Derby Road were purchased from Zion Mills in 1901. Alton's 'Kingston Club Special' cigars were made from tobacco imported from Jamaica. Alton's Corvanna cigars were introduced in the 1930s, when the weekly wage for a worker would have been 11s. This factory closed in 1990.

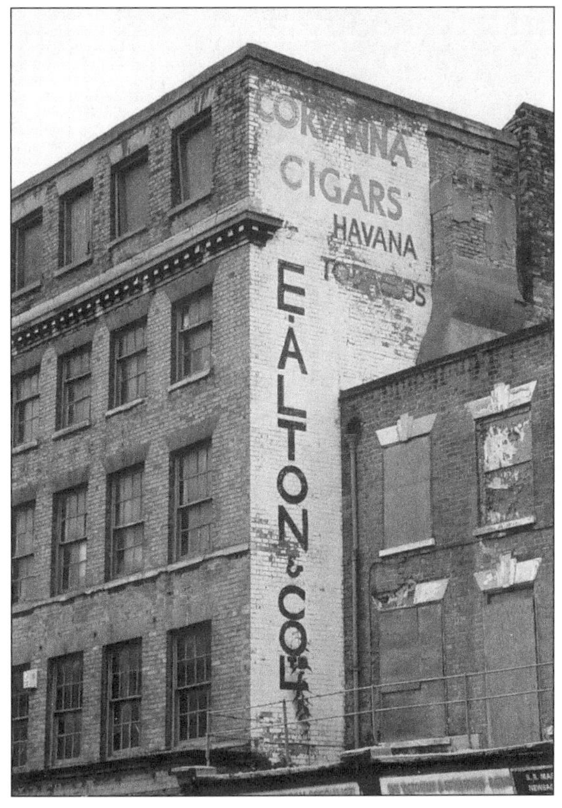

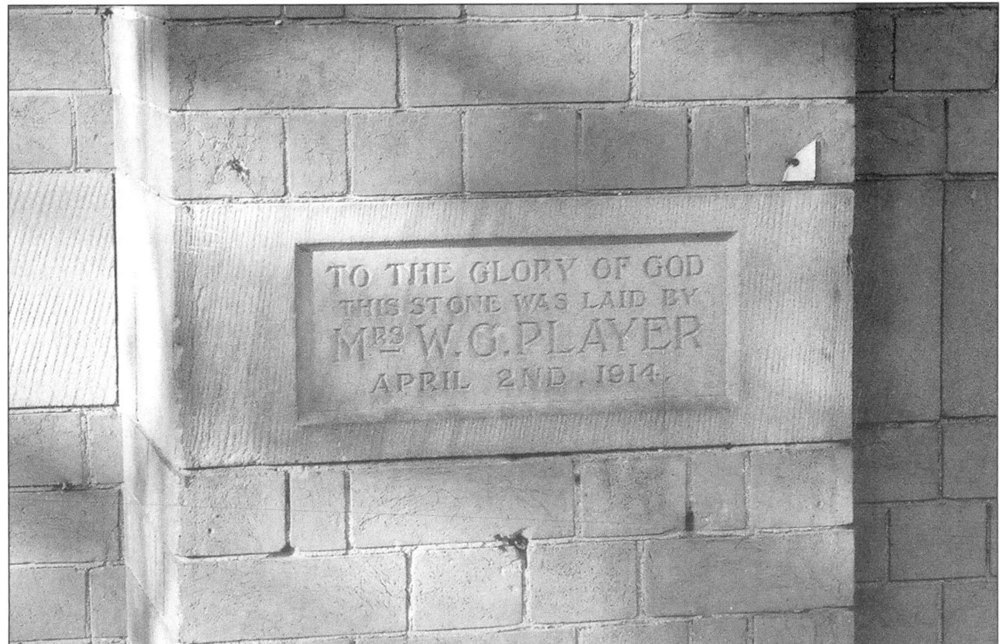

Plaque, Lenton Boulevard, 1991. Mrs William Goodacre Player, wife of the owner of John Player & Sons, laid this stone. It is located on the former chapel building next to Radford and Lenton Library, formerly a piano workshop.

Teleradio shop, 207 Ilkeston Road, 1984. At some stage in its history, this shop had been Kirk's barbers and a toyshop, but had been a radio dealers since 1950. The chip shop in the picture was formerly Bostock and Tyson's fish friers.

Temples Newsagents, Alfreton Road, 1988. Before this newsagent's at 174 Alfreton Road was taken over by Frank Temple, it was a confectioner's shop, leased in 1895 by H. Riley & Sons.

Memorial stone for Bramcote Street United Methodist chapel, 1992. A similar stone at the front bears the date 6 May 1878. J.W. Priestley was a Radford builder, based on Norton Street.

No. 13 Croydon Road, 1980. The door number on Victorian housing was normally painted in black copperplate script onto a brick adjacent to the doorway. Overly ornate letterbox flaps and doorknockers (here absent) were also features applied by the builders in the 1880s.

Gatepost in Forest Road West. This sturdy combination of stone and ironwork was built sometime before 1880, which led to Waterloo Promenade, mainly home to lace, cycle and iron workers, between the wars. The Nottingham Institute for the Deaf was located on Forest Road West in the 1920s, as were Young's Monumental Masons and Hunt's Furniture Directors.

Roof of Coronato's ice cream manufacturers, Medway Street, 1990. This ancient lettering dates back to around 1940, when F.G. Pearce owned the factory on Medway Street, although by 1956 he had relocated to nearby Grant Street.

Barnett's Confectioners, Cobden Street, 1982. The product being advertised here is the 'Barnips' cough sweet, a small extra-strong black lozenge, which along with 'Stormguards', helped Radford residents through many a harsh winter. Most of Cobden Street, along with Butler Street, Guthrie Street, Stansfield Street, and Scarcliffe Terrace, was removed in the Salisbury Street clearance programme of 1978. This building, however, has survived.

Cast-iron sign outside Raleigh Industries, Triumph Road factory, 1990. This feature now stands in front of the last remaining Radford cycle works, and dates from 1952. However, this factory is scheduled to close in the next few years, sadly ending its Radford association.

Advertisement for Taylor's coal merchants, Hartley Road, 1998. The sign is actually referring to Samuel Taylor, Coal Dealer, at 48 Denison Street, across the road, and dates from the 1940s. However, the modern CCTV cameras do not aid its traditional appeal!

Coronato's Ice Cream advertisement, Wollaton Road, 1995. Two Italian brothers, Vincent and Eddie Coronato, started this Medway Street business in 1971. Today Eddie's son Luigi carries on the family tradition.

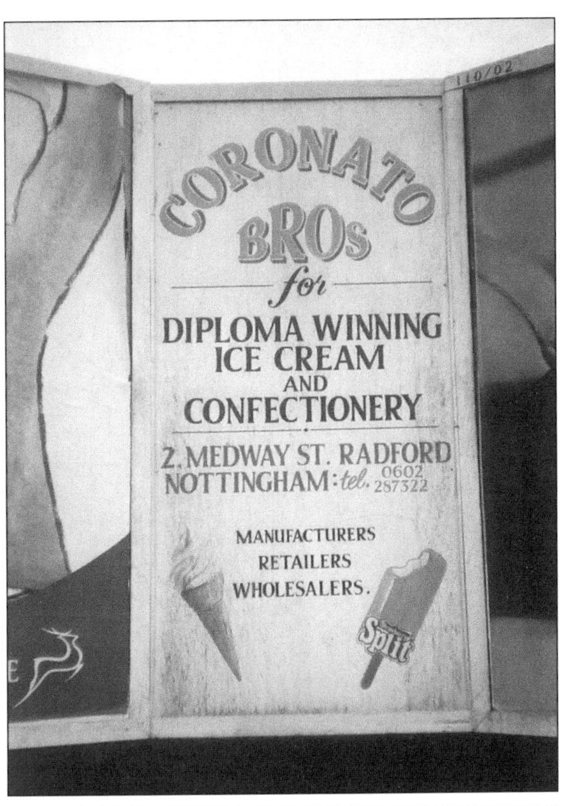

Hairdresser's sign, Hartley Road, 1982. This ingenious method of advertising is actually referring to Stokes' Barbers across the road, formerly Dunn's Men's Hairdressers. The junction in the distance is Alfreton Road.

Gatling Street sign, 1988. Gatling Street, Rifle Street, Bastion Street and Target Street were all named with a military theme in mind. The Gatling gun was patented in America in 1862 and saw action during the Civil War.

Sign for William Hollins and Co., Garden Street, 1984. This old silk mill dates from 1897, and was formerly a clothing warehouse, which was used in the Second World War for soldiers' billets and for the reconditioning of Spitfire Merlin engines.

Vernon's butchers sign, Stansfield Street, 1995. This shop was near the Cobden Billiards Hall on Ilkeston Road, which became a YMCA and then a youth club, Rad-Y, set up in the 1960s by Ray Woodhouse.

The Boulevard Works, 1996. This building has few plaques or clues to its history; this one is located on Radford Boulevard, and has been placed over one of the entrance gates.

Lettering above Raleigh Canteen building, 1996. This feature was part of the Raleigh Social Club and Canteen building seen on p. 48, which has now been demolished to make way for buildings for the University of Nottingham.

Gambles factory, Newdigate Street, 1997. This impressive factory, now derelict, was once the home of the Vertex Hosiery Repair Service, G.T. Hussey & Co., blouse manufacturers, and the Mayfair Manufacturing Company, among others.

Nine

Then and Now

Newsagent's shop, 91 Ilkeston Road, 2000. The new sign on the corner of Balfour Road has been ripped away to reveal the ancient 'John Player' script underneath it. In 1941, this shop was kept by Edith Stevens, newsagent.

Hartley Road, 1984. The clock on the wall belongs to the Hartley Road post office, which in 1901 was known as a 'Branch Post, Money Order and Counting Office'. Nearby was the popular ladies' shop 'Vanity Fayre'.

Hartley Road, 2000. Much has changed in twenty years: the shops in this picture now include a Jamaican café, Dels 4 Bargains second-hand shop, and Jordan's Pharmacy, relocated from the old Bird's chemists shop on Denman Street, which has now fallen into disrepair.

Brixton Road, 1982. Here, the Plough pub is still owned by Whitbread. In 1982, a terraced house on this street could be purchased for just £9,000. After the Second World War, however, one could have been acquired for as little as £50.

The Plough, St Peter's Street, 1999. This pub had a £30,000 refurbishment in 1985, when the licensees were Paul and Brenda Flint. The building dates from 1932, although an inn of this name is listed on the site in the 1830s.

Fryma Fabrics, Denison Street, 1982. In the 1980s, Fryma was the UK's largest exporter of knitted industrial mesh fabric. This building was nicknamed 'Farmer Faggots' by local children, and was closed in 1992.

Denison Street, 2000. New housing has now been since built on the Fryma site and the ancient factory wall has been disguised with greenery.

Forster Street Café, 1982. Radford has been home to many coffee bars: Marian's Café on Ilkeston Road, Leonardi's on Denman Street, and Irene's Café at 139 Hartley Road are just some which have passed into memory.

A café on Forster Street, 2000. The outside of this building has now fallen into disrepair, its red paintwork cracked and peeling. The derelict shops in the distance belong to Denman Street and were formerly Ellen Dumpleton's drapers and Mackley's greengrocers.

Demolition of the Raleigh factory on Faraday Road, 1990. It is seen from the River Leen side of the road. This factory originally housed sixteen gas engines, had a frontage of 520ft, and was used for the making of munitions during the Second World War.

New housing, Faraday Road, 2000. Kittiwake Mews and Heron Drive are two of the new streets in this development, built on the site of the first Raleigh factory on Faraday Road.

Car on Gatling Street, 1980. During hot summers in the 1930s, the tar between the cobbles would bubble, and children would be encouraged to breathe the fumes from the tar wagons as a cure for whooping cough. The houses on the left are 2-8 Gatling Street.

Gatling Street, 2000. The cobbles have now been asphalted over and two decades of weather have eroded the stone-rendered backyard wall. The new properties in the distance belong to a rebuilt Citadel Street.

Denman Street, 1982. Anderson's pawnshop had just moved here into the former Skelton's electrical stores, from 298-302 Denman Street, which had been pulled down. A hundred years before, the Ford's drapers stores had been Bishop's pikelet bakers and confectioners.

Denman Street, 2000. The old pawnbroker's shop has long since been converted into housing, with an ornate brickwork corner. Holland's shop in the centre was once a newsagents owned by Florence Jessop.

Butcher's shop on Beresford Street, 1982. The final customer is being served on a chilly winter's day. There were many notable Denman Street butchers, some famous ones being Albert Bailey, Ernest Croft, Harry Dickens, Tom Evley, Preston's and Scrimshaw's.

Beresford Street, 2000. Like its partner on the opposite corner of this street (see p. 124), this shop has also been converted into a house. The old Radford Fisheries (fish and game) shop was located where the lamppost is standing on the right.

Faraday Road, 1988. This shop was previously Edna Ball's grocer's shop at the corner of Cycle Road. A more detailed photograph of the clock on the bridge can be seen on p. 52.

Faraday Road, 2000. Houses and a children's nursery now occupy the site of the Raleigh road bridge. Michael Faraday, the famous nineteenth-century inventor, lent his name to this street.

Cycle Road, 1989. The main feature here is the Raleigh three-speed gear assembly shop on the left, demolished in 1990. This revolutionary cycle gear was patented in 1902, and was invented by Henry Sturmey and James Archer.

Cycle Road, 2000. In the distance is Johnson Road and the district of Lenton. Most of the terraced houses on the right were not constructed until at least 1897, the road being named after the adjacent bicycle factory.

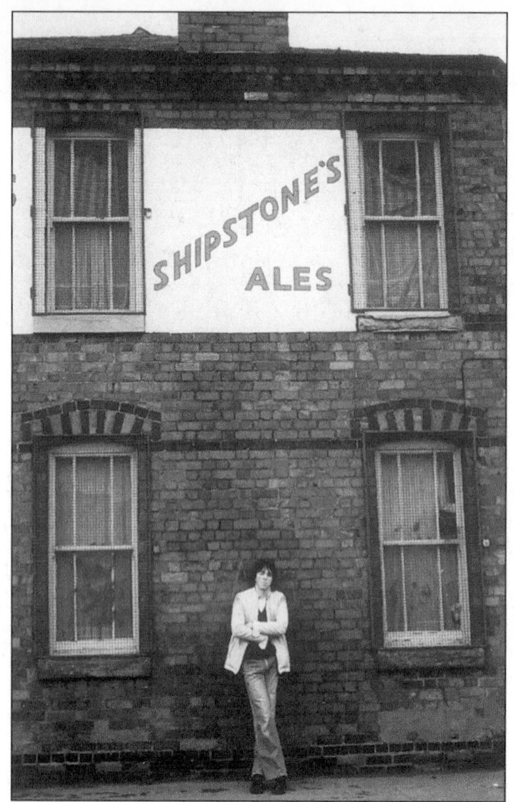

Chris Richards, aged seventeen in Dorset Street, 1979. No. 71 Dorset Street was an off-licence occupied by Joseph and Hilda Wilson, inevitably selling Shipstone's Gold Star, Nut Brown and India Pale Ale. In 1950, it was a grocer's shop belonging to Annie Chambers.

No. 71 Dorset Street, 2000. Most of the streets in this area, such as Canterbury Road and Bridport Avenue, were named after regions of Southern England and were built between 1883 and 1885. Twenty-one years have taken their toll on the building, and the author's waistline!